Artist and Model

Artist and Model

Carol Snow

THE ATLANTIC MONTHLY PRESS
NEW YORK

Copyright © 1990 by Carol Snow

All rights reserved. No part of this book may be reproduced in any form or by any electronic or mechanical means including information storage and retrieval systems without permission in writing from the publisher, except by a reviewer, who may quote brief passages in a review.

Published simultaneously in Canada
Printed in the United States of America
FIRST EDITION

Library of Congress Cataloging-in-Publication Data

Snow, Carol.
    Artist and model / Carol Snow.—1st ed.
    ISBN 0-87113-400-4
    I. Title.
    PS3569.N57A88   1990   811'.54—dc20   90-45060

The Atlantic Monthly Press
19 Union Square West
New York, NY 10003

Design by Laura Hough

FIRST PRINTING

*For David, Kathy, Laura,
and for my family.*

Acknowledgments

Grateful acknowledgment is made to the editors of the following publications, in which versions of these poems originally appeared: *The American Poetry Review:* "Bridge"; *Antaeus:* "Positions of the Body"; *Berkeley Poetry Review:* "[The Upward Is Endless]"; *Denver Quarterly:* "Artist and Model III," "Artist and Model IV," "Artist and Model V"; *Pavement:* "Since Particles"; *Pequod:* "Aria," "Mourner's *Kasen* (Mourner's Series)," "Prospect *(The Graces)*"; *Verse:* "The Back of the White Blouse," *"Le Déjeuner,"* "Trees We Pass."

My gratitude also to the San Francisco Foundation for the Joseph Henry Jackson Award in Literature, 1985, granted for this manuscript in progress.

Fragments of poems quoted in "Aria" and "Bridge" are from "Duino Elegies" by Rainer Maria Rilke, "Of Being Numerous" by George Oppen, and "Canto IV" by Ezra Pound (*The Collected Poems of George Oppen* and *The Cantos of Ezra Pound* were both published by New Directions Publishing Corporation).

References to photographs of and statements by Henri Matisse in the "Artist and Model" poems are from *The Artists of My Life,* Brassaï (New York: Viking Penguin, Inc., 1982) and *Matisse on Art,* Jack D. Flam (New York: Phaidon Press Limited, 1973).

Primary reference (and inspiration) for the form of "Mourner's *Kasen* (Mourner's Series)" was *Monkey's Raincoat: Linked Poetry of the Basho School with Haiku Selections* (Japan: Charles E. Tuttle Company, Inc., 1985), translated and with an Introduction by Lenore Mayhew.

Contents

Positions of the Body

Prospect (The Graces)   3
Positions of the Body   5
[The Upward Is Endless]   17
Aria   18
Two Forms   22

Artist and Model

Artist and Model I: The House Opposite   27
Artist and Model II: After Daphne   28
Artist and Model III: The Morning Exercise   29
Artist and Model IV: From the Model   31
Artist and Model V: Likeness   32
Artist and Model VI: Artist and Model   34

Frame

The Back of the White Blouse   37
Frame   38
Two Lyrics   39

Short Poem   40
Since Particles   41
Mourner's Kasen (Mourner's Series)   43

Poems After Monet

Living in Venice   53
Le Déjeuner   55
Trees We Pass   57
Bridge   58

Note on "*Mourner's Kasen (Mourner's Series)*"   65
Biographical Note   67

POSITIONS OF THE BODY

Prospect (The Graces)

At this distance,
space accumulates color—the luminous
blue of dusk acknowledging water, the water
a flatness so vast it seems to acquire height. And the mountains

bordering are without shadow or chiaroscuro—such black
solidity at this distance, I am
what: an eye; attention? abstraction?
Null if I do not speak? This distance?

*

Blackness against sea, against sky.
Mass refuting ascent, descent,
the feathered, the molten, the scattered;
against movement in water
    (the repeated breaking of surface).
                      Blackness
as solace so I waited
(as if I were distance) to give voice.
A blackness out of that privacy and silence we drown in.

*

Here are the Graces (this was said clearly):
Distance, Wash, Solidity—
                              the mountainous coast, black
and deafening or such that everything else fell silent.

Density, presence, stress—that Solidity;—
breath, not as wind and not rising and falling
pulled at weak edges like the sea,
but breath as a voice rising and falling.

Positions of the Body

I

Above the Crucifixion,

above the Lamentation, Giotto's angels hang
griefstruck against worn sky.
You can see they are inconsolable—in their
attitudes of suffering
                or suffering-with:
backs taut, hands flung
open or rending or mutely clasped; the gestures
carried to apogee—held

without comfort
              (since comfort is a learned thing).

*

The girl, held
in the ward, distracted and

failing, not blind, tried to study
Braille for solace

in the dark, for other
voices into sleep.

    And when a voice she could not stop
hearing carried her

onto her feet—as if footprints were painted on the floor:
one step forward, one step back,

one step forward, one step back—that two-step also

hoped for something.

Not by a desperate discarding of positions;

rather as though the body recalled
safety or moments of adequate praise

or grace,
  brief and shifting.

11

As half-asleep, one arm
bent, fist to the lips, both
legs together and folded up

into the empty reaches, head
pressed to the pillow, eyes closed, you know the world
as the blessing of clean dry cloth only;

or above the yard waving in the coming
rush of afternoon, the fervent
dampness of hems and your leaning
against the porch rail by the laundry line

seem consonant offerings.

As sitting in a truck stop off the highway,
late summer, leaning toward

the picture window, elbows convinced
of the tabletop, hands believing a cup of hot tea,
you watched the trees by a filling station

becoming more deeply green and you felt such immense
gratitude for light it explained the leaves' arching.

III

The slender twisting of green
stems through water in a glass vase
set on a table of the museum café

transfixed you; yet afterward, not the clasping
of your hands or your legs' crossing or even
the image survived, but your wanting that beauty

in you, contained in you.

IV

The ill-shaven man is in profile,

lips puckered, arms outstretched
in a gesture of embrace so the bearded man,
all but his face, is hidden by the yellow robe—the
    verticals

of torches above them, the fanning
of clubs and spears that helmeted men
wield across sky. (Masts,

shifting at the marina, angle
and cross like that—abstract
and perfect as the balance Giotto

has captured in fresco: beyond fable or ritual
    embodiment;
beyond the expression on Christ's face
or on Judas's face, as their eyes meet.)

                                    Visitors
line the Arena Chapel, crowded
before the artist's work: they are still

and lost to themselves for a while; shifting;
lost for a while and still.

                    v

She stands in a scattered crowd of herself—the
     model
in the sculpture studio of L'Académie Julian, Rue
     du Dragon,

Paris. It is 1931 and Brassaï is there; his camera
     has noted
the sober, mustachioed artists, the heroic

expressions of busts on a shelf above her,
the frieze of plaster nudes in various

classical poses.
                    How naked she seems. Standing
there she knows she possesses almost nothing—
     position

only—and the men,
taking that knowledge from her face to touch the
clay of her body without desire,

        touch desire
in themselves they cannot give up.

VI

Wanting not only the stillness of hills,
but intercession—as by new grass

on the hills—with the silence
towering over the hills, Moore sculpts a massive

figure in black marble: a woman's
body, reclining, curved; eloquent

as bone, shell,
stones worn beyond contradiction.

*

        You stopped
by the roadside, hills

lying in middle distance, few houses. Only the green
reaches of vineyard intervening

seemed manageable; that is, human—a matter
of scale; the silence was huge, so that only

the hills (which were huge,
also) could rest.

Cézanne, leaning to his canvas, would have mastered
that view, you thought: the blues and greens
and ochres of proximity and distance; that tenuous

position in the dance, not of the drawing
together of unlike, like bodies, but of the holding
apart of the body and terrain; you were held

so still, you thought that you might become those hills,
or must have been borne by hills,

or maybe your body
had been a maquette for the hills.

VII

In *Mother and Child (Pietà)*—the bronze

figures not only entwined, but contiguous—
Kollwitz expresses deep grief

as stillness: this woman wants, in her,
the hills, to become

stone with her child;
the shape of embrace is everything to her.

And circling that terrible desire
to stop, you have no name for a moment; your hand lifts
to your mouth like the twisting

to light
       of grass and new leaves.

VIII

                           You had wanted to go back, to
    step
back in time, through art: before *Guernica*;
The Raft of the Medusa; *Executions of 3rd May, 1808*;

before the weight of Christ's body,
failing the rigid geometry of the cross,
documented suffering.
                    You stood
in the duecento, expecting icon only—the body
abstracted, formal, schematic—and Giotto
had chosen a greenish cast for the skin,

straining the upheld arms, skewing
the wounded torso and bent legs, bowing forward
the still face: Word made flesh, not stylized; dead
weight to be lifted down, angels writhing.

So the exhumation of murdered nuns

in El Salvador, priests and cameras
called to a makeshift grave (you had watched
in tarnished light): how the bodies

                                      were awkwardly moved
(your hands clasped tightly together),
how they tangled and did not cover themselves.

IX

And Milosz keeps talking about the dead.
His dead, whom you never would have known;
you are beginning to know their shadows

as you know the position of your body on the bed:
half-awake, one arm
bent to your head, feet turned in a little awkwardly

in summer morning—
its light through closed eyelids,
its hammering

from a yard beyond the yard beyond
the window past the rice-paper shade.
An engine turns over. A dog's barking. Someone has come out

onto a landing; faintly you hear
loud laughter, imagine his leaning toward the succession
of gardens you have begun to see—

near sleep—as the portraits of Ambroise Vollard;
variations on one garden; recurrent
memory.

X

      The body, remembering
exile, apprehends

suffering, carries the anguished, impossible
angle of panicked flight of the woman
caught in Picasso's *Guernica*
                      (another woman—her shrill
tongue a knife-edged scream she cannot loose, her child
dripping from her arms—raises
a tiny palm in her palm; and someone keeps
burning, probably—hands splayed, eyes, face: everything pushing
upward): the body—

dazed, in a debt of tears, a pale
cartoon of grief—offers expressive
gestures, importunate gestures;

so that when there is no comfort, there is this: the willful
body making its signs for comfort—

*

Say you were never that girl, taken and
nameless, held mute in a dwindling
litany of positions; your body

knows how her body would speak to her
of comfort, sometimes—

proffering embraces or touching
her face—how grieving

for her, the body
                curled to become a seed.

[The Upward Is Endless]

The upward is endless.
                    Sky, I mean: distance, rooted
among houses and trees, tangled in daylight
across a desk and down the inverted
spines of open books. And though gratitude sometimes
wells up, it is also like water in that it rises
upon itself . . .

            I watch a yellow chair—or rather,
watch the measurable distance to the chair—a little uncertain
even among belongings. The chill
on my skin is like fine silt, something failed
in rising but through which I move freely
        so it cannot be lifted.
                        Maybe it is gratitude
I fear—the weight of it, flooding

into the external skeleton (this world
of things, I mean: bookshelves, rooms and window frames; fences,
the branches and leaves of trees) and struggling

upward.

Aria

You've hung out the wash, so the wind plays out in wetness and
    dryness
        the evening-out

death is: the desire
in things for stasis that dictates wind.
                              Grass and leaves rustle
in the wind and sunlight (the steadily arriving
wind with which everything
green and breathing transacts to continue). A cat
stalks a low feeding—

        . . . The cat—

        . . . One of the cats
stalks a low feeding, the laundry swinging; hydrangeas nearby, and
    bougainvillea, and roses
spilling over the fence from a neighbor's yard:
                              light, spilled

over; and leaves, the innumerable angles of facing that light.
". . . And he fails! He fails, that meditative man! And indeed they
    cannot 'bear' it": you hear Oppen's voice.

                                        Or the voice of a
        tape of his voice you have listened to
over and over for the words' singing (the words a singing
even without meaning), singing even without meaning; singing,
and even without meaning—*Denn das Schöne ist nichts / als des
        Schrecklichen Anfang* . . .—

                                . . . light, spilled

over, the yards
turning through spilled light so the light
pitches and wind

rises with the increasing angle
of light and you usually go in about this time.

You've hung out the wash, so the wind plays out in wetness and
        dryness
                the evening-out

death is: the breaking-down
going on under weeds and light
spilled from the sun's breaking—the light
slanting; the wind coming up, a passing
by; hydrangeas near-

by, and bougainvillea, and roses
spilling over the fence from a neighbor's yard—
    not toward you.
               But you turn the world toward you.

    As, driving the hills to work—not up Franklin (which has
        timed lights, so you're intent on making the lights, and
        pedestrians
waiting to cross look past you as though you were wind or
        already past), but over
a steeper route toward the bay (at Kathy's, talking to Kathy,
        you watch her face; when she turns toward the window,
        the side of her face, then her face; she holds a white,
        blue and yellow
Monet morning cup of coffee. The objects in the room, as
        though faceted,
at each angle you hold still, have faces toward you)—you tilt
        the bay
more and less toward you: just over the highest stop—like a
        lover, over; that angle (Kathy
drinks from her coffee, the garden through the window; if you
        look down you *can* see the tabletop)—the bay almost
in plan—

        . . . and bougainvillea, and roses
spilling over the fence from a neighbor's yard. You sit
with that. With the greenness
and breathing by which you continue (not *for* you), wind

rising which is beginning dusk, the gorgeous
flowers gorgeous to continue
                              (the beauty
of that).

Two Forms

THERE IS MASTERY

of emptiness: birds

ploughing great arcs of migration across the invisible
bending at Earth's curve; the warmth of each hollow-boned body
held by the air
              held in the branching
filaments branching

from a thousand hollow quills.

THERE IS ALREADY

agreement between us

in the use of words. That we categorize. Have shattered the world
for the sake of resemblances.
                                      Poet and reader—
we inhabit, in passing,
one body: of lost correspondences; a joining

of words that proposes the world is divided
—of *Light*—

oh not irreparably.

ARTIST AND MODEL

Artist and Model I

THE HOUSE OPPOSITE

I sit on my bed, something amiss, the house opposite filling my
    window
with slats and stairs and railings; the glare
of this time of day from the white face—
it shifts a little when I tilt my head—
throws the familiar surroundings into shadow.

                                      I could go to the
    window,
where half the world is sky and that face
is only a house in a row of houses—but one I saw painted white,
so that we are betrothed, I think. I will not move,
will not lose this size.

                        I will sit on my bed, the house
opposite—struts and light and Picasso's
eyes, I think, those dark windows—and want to sleep.
And want to be watched sleeping.

Artist and Model II

AFTER DAPHNE

I saw the houses across the street and thought *paper dolls*;
a picket fence; *the innocence*

of repetition because houses
have no business wounding me.
                              Not pleasure; I did not take
    pleasure in

the angles and planes which man makes, that light
shared by the painted surfaces—
light glancing from flat panes
of glass wantonly; ruthlessly, almost—rather they took me

beyond pleasure: the houses alike
and touching.
              I wanted refuge; and thought to take refuge—in

fence or *alike* or the dark of these dark
trees—as Daphne took flight.

Artist and Model III

THE MORNING EXERCISE

"It is my habit
always to return to nature," Matisse told Brassaï.

                                              So the branches
and leaves set in a pitcher the artist
studies, in one of the photographs:

                                    branches—
already almost line—and leaves—

surface—Matisse will draw (will reduce
to line) as his morning exercise.
                              ". . . not just a question of
copying this branch, but of creating something equivalent to
it."

*

What is the motive force of a branch—
                                  the forming

of tree from which it was taken? the idea

of *tree*, of *reach*;
to branch? to break into leaf? And of leaves—

                                              surface, sense;
transaction (of light

and air and water, their greenness creating
equivalents)?
        (The morning exercise.)

Artist and Model IV

FROM THE MODEL

The attention he gives to her, here in the photograph
    (Matisse—"One must always search for the desire of the line,
                        where it wishes
to enter or where to die away. Also always be sure of its source;
    this must be done from the model"), his surroundings—
the painting on an easel in the foreground; behind him, a pitcher
    of branches
and leaves; couch,
chest, trochee, dactyl and dactyl—forgotten (overtaken
as he is by a curve of thigh): creating

a sign for her ("I will condense the meaning of this body by
    seeking
its essential lines"),
                  to some extent he becomes her—the volume
and curves of her—as he has set her (standing, ankles crossed,
    breasts lifted—
the back is arched, the arms encircling her head; which is slightly
turned and looking

downward); she has granted him that.

Artist and Model V

LIKENESS

She slices the pear,

                    and pear falls in white slabs
flat and blank as the fronts of houses
she faces sometimes and feels mirrored, her fingers
barely pressing the tender place below her eye
(where time happens),
                      yet resting on the bone sill
under—not flesh, not trembling: still
as houses.
        The slices,
she lifts cleanly to her mouth, the pear not bitten—her mouth
not having made a crater the shape of her mouth in the white
pear and the crater flooding; nor her mouth
flooding to answer its sweetness. She wants that sweetness

contained: to taste it and not be moved
to speak—so fearing the tenderness
of her body held open to pleasure;

                                        in that incompleteness
    sometimes,
a voice moving the air presses her.

Artist and Model VI

ARTIST AND MODEL

It is all here in the photograph
of Matisse and the dark-haired model I resemble: the artist—
portly, white-bearded, bespectacled (in 1939, almost seventy)—
presaging my father (in 1939, my father was smiling my smile for
    his high school photograph.
I remember that picture; I studied that picture: I know I resemble
    my father). Matisse
resembles, is not, my father; the white smock over his vest and tie,
sketchbook open on one knee, a pitcher of branches and leaves
behind him, Matisse has found a surface
the line desires and regards a span of the woman's body with
    possessive attention
or gratitude, not madness. And I think that I cannot be
or desire my father—being Matisse;

                                that is, having for this
    complexity
of resemblance the passion Matisse had for line, for that curve
of thigh I see myself balancing book and paper against.

FRAME

The Back of the White Blouse

The back of the white blouse, buttoned with white buttons
—or the woman's back
filling the white blouse—
so the buttons strained at the buttonholes
and pleats were made:
I sat behind that all through the reading.

I'd been trying to describe how being outdoors
seemed easy—leaves and grass
attending to being green as a kind of company;—how my difficulty
living alone was exacerbated by objects
I had chosen or been given, by their continually having to be
    recognized
—which, like the doll's
staying with me all night tenderly,
I knew as a conceit.

Frame

A composition is in the sliding mirror (so the edges of the world
weren't necessary after all!): with the vertical bar between window
    frames, then the cleft house and its neighbor
(but set in deep space)—framed, each behind a tree—fronted by a
    bird at the feeder
on the sill. *Outside.* A bright sky.
And glare, the reflected light from some pale siding in particular,
so that the series of birds feeding is a shadow repeating the shape
    of the (shadowed) figurine
on the sill—*in here*—but an animate shadow.
A print and a painting on the wall by the windows.

This much of a bicycle: foreshortened handlebars, a section of
    pitchfork
of frame, a shallow arc of wheel, a bike lock hanging from the
    handlebars
(all this upside down). I am hidden behind the file cabinet;
the bicycle is hanging from the ceiling but you will not know that.
We are not allowing the whole of the bicycle
in here.

Two Lyrics

AND WHEN WE EMBRACE

　　　　　　　　—the fours of
hands and arms and shoulders

and legs, and the two
torsos; but only

your face.

DAVID, WHEN WE EMBRACE

　　　　　　　—such
foreshortening!

Short Poem

Hurrying past
a dog in a parked car:
arf ARF arf.

Since Particles

1.
If ten double and twelve simple letters made a world.
And atoms were smashed of that world.
If ă.

(But open mouths; the repetition of open mouths, numinous.)

2.
Words for objects not used.

                    That is,
words for objects used but the objects not used,
so the words become objects. Not used.

3.
Open the box. The words open the box.
Inside the box the words open the box.
Inside the box the words Inside the box the words open the box.
Be romantic.

4.
'Withered'.

Less 'over' than 'fields'.

The point. Or only
(since particles) fragment.

Mourner's *Kasen*
(Mourner's Series)

for Kaela Petrov-Levine (1920–1987)

Uncertain

what I am going to do—

I am going to move from here to there.

Here where the world is engaged.

'Here' and 'there' in the withheld description.

In that 'progression', what one approaches is moving toward; what one passes,

away.

". . . passes, // away" makes me made me think *when she died* . . .—
pathos of the feminine, of the lost (dependent- or maternal-possible?)—

For that woman—the lecturer said—the picture
of a fish—I pictured—was fear, was her lost
innocence, was "a hole in 'the real'."

Not knowing the fish would be eaten—

the goldfish I bought for the oak-barrel tub—(by a cat? by
    raccoons?).

Lap swimming at the community pool:

the woman in front of me—the soles of her feet—like an angel
on some rococo ceiling, dangling from (ascending straight into)
    Heaven.

From one eye, the lover's nose and chin;
from the other, his chin and the window.

Daybreak—
the sky through flowering branches;
there is a loneliness to point of view.

In the painting Cézanne had made several proposals
concerning the placed outline of a barn.

And . . . *you lost her completely* keeps retreating
further and further behind—left
behind in one of the many places a particular

life against 'ground' might end.

Move a little to the left and see that.

In the morning, between neighborhood hills,

the grays of downtown (once
or from time to time) almost lost in haze.

For some time after his (second) wife died, Monet
"could not bear to face the motif."

Yes, the light (in passing). Yes,
the garden—illumined—remembered in the water

(during).

Kaela as memories only—as reflection:—

dependent, disjunct, desultory.

Words painted on the street, reading
AHEAD WAY ONE from 'top' to 'bottom';
ONE WAY AHEAD as you come to them.

A prospect, a windshield, a face;

series, a beginning to locate.

Prospect—

always arriving
here inexpressible in detail.

"Come *on*": in a voice so mean,
the little boy must have been her brother.

In the street by the curb—
scattered glass.

Kaela, are you missing the cruelty?

*Her eyes, closed, and her mouth,
closed.*

In water in the tub, in the lapses—between the protuberance
of breasts and the protuberance of knees—where the
'recalling-as' of the fixtures, is . . . (you must be dreaming).

Ranks of mountains, emerging
through ranks of mist.

Trees could be seen from the road—
a clear cut? a lake, beyond?—
as a screen of trees.

A tree stepped out from a tree and began to accompany me: image

or ghost (poor ghost without surface, through which light changes).

Now Kaela often sits as she was
sitting that day by her window. Wasted but happy
to see me, she looks

beautiful—I never saw her (went to see her)
again because of that.

"Blanche!" The light has changed; Monet's stepdaughter
brings the painter the requisite canvas in progress (image, fixed in
    one light—

oh memory).

Motif is 'to rest in'.

Grief—grief is 'to wander'.

In the oak-barrel tub
a hungry goldfish
gulps the littered surface through its o.

Daylight—yards, backs of houses, storage shed;
detail bored deeply into the moments.

Detail, survived
by words (as by brushstrokes)—vague and summary:—
'buildings', 'trees', 'distance' . . .

'A distance', 'the distance', 'that distance', 'this distance':
as, to approach or to embrace.

Still to embrace

[a, the, that, this]
world without motif—

Kaela—
all this in your absence.

POEMS
AFTER
MONET

Living in Venice

(Like)

reflections of boats—like boats, erasures
of sky moved in the bay in the harbor (inversions of white
hulls, the red of a
keel, blue

shadows of blue sail covers: color

dangled in the rhythm of the water)—leached
in the pulled blue-green of the depth of the water, masts
ribboned. Tattered. Like the bright shapes between dark shapes of
    poplars poured from the base of a stand of poplars—
interstices, sky, foliage, clouds,
trunks, distance as surface (like the birds—

snowy egrets? arctic terns? whose name I didn't bother to
    remember—I remembered from a nature film—
they were swallowing water—when the ducks at the zoo were
    swallowing water: bills turned up and the white vibrato of
    throat—and laughed—ecstatic; like laughter) which wavers,
    which gathers
like the bureau repainted
flat black and glossy black
that will not be solid in memory.

                        A woman
thinks she belongs in a bathtub—
thighs obscured by the soapy water,
the water warmer than hands or kisses—
watching, over the tangle of black crotch-hair, a square of light
    (from the light in the bathroom window above her) she
    cannot hold still enough.
Which shudders, like . . .

                    (Which shudders, is my reflection.)

Le Déjeuner

A still life: on a table, a white paper
napkin in a spill of water. The remains
of a sandwich, a salad (two plates).
                                      Objects—

napkins, a glass
of some water, flatware, sugar bowl, coffee cup—
(some as at rest on a journey through, some
stationed as at a station on their circuits of,
the café)
           for the moment as form on the form of an outdoor table.

I told him briefly of that hard time, my eyes fixed
on the table (watching the teaspoon
on a napkin near my hand, the water glass,

the bowl of little packets of sweetener and sugar
not changed or harmed).

*

Not to look up at concern (his face);
                                    and a couple walking away
from a vendor's booth across the street
with the freshly squeezed orange juice they'd paid for; and traffic,
and litter, maybe a stray; a woman at a neighboring table,

nodding. And the order rustling of the letters of the names of the
    forms of the masses
of blades of leaves moving in the texture of the mass of the figures
of trees I might see growing behind him east of campus (his eyes
    alarmed).

I would leave you with the objects on the table

as he and I arranged them: the paper napkin crumpled in the
    water spilled
from my setting down my glass of water nervously, the
    wheat-colored cup he cupped in one hand, plates of the last
    pieces of lettuce and the crusts of his BLT—curves of the
    plates, of the empty cup, of the handle and bowl of the spoon
    at my place (weighting a napkin still folded from the
    dispenser) glinting
dully in the sun, marked as they were by many uses and
    washings—objects
left on a table.

        Objects on a table
in a season, at a time of day.

Trees We Pass

Our going on driving to Kathy's and my looking out the window
fell in a silence after
the silence which followed
difficult words—and evenings of easier
words and other
silences following . . . the sweetness of our having met, that
    embrace—
continued our opening new time.

It is not enough to paint these trees in this light.

Bridge

1) *IL MIGLIOR FABBRO*

And jumped up "to make tea," he said: an old man, having
    forgotten
rest—he couldn't "get flat enough"—kept lying down

and jumping up "to make tea"
(habit as the shell the husk the hull of mastery).

> —Tension building in my shoulders aspiring to the grandeur of
>   classical architecture (a Parthenon
> or Temple of Athena Nike): noble but archaic—static, L. said—
> the arch and the vault unknown.

> —Changes in the flesh of a woman's body, described (as are hills'
>   curves
> by my drive over them to work) by instances over time of the
>   motions of a bath towel over arms, shoulders, belly, breasts,
> calves, thighs, crotch, buttocks, feet, in some usual order.

> —A face only, wanting to emerge from water, making
> a mask of the surface of the water, the surface
> tension of the water unbroken
>
>   (is it an eye I mean? reflective and

> *turning as toward prey—a man and two women standing at*
> *the railing of the Japanese footbridge*
> *arched above and over the pond—*
> *each thing seen, of the garden, shaken?)*

And lapsed into silence, but a long silence.

*

As from no vantage.

From more than a darkness of eyes closed—
as from eyes closed in the darkness of a closed box.

Wanting the expression of no-face.
Not to speak not even to speak
tonelessly and without emphasis.

To go deeply into a flat dream of surface.

> *—Water in the pond as that which has fallen (has found a level);*
> *visages of garden, bridge, sky (supine and contingent—*
> *collapsed on the skin of the surface) as its Heavenly firmament.*

Flat. Flat! (Without affect.)

2) BRIDGE:

That I sat on a lawn between the houses—trees between the
    houses
unfamiliar, Eastern trees—between warm rains, alone

for a while, alone yet at ease as though 'in company': leaves
and the grass going on being green—or you could say

gods were there, ". . . Choros nympharum, goat-foot, with the pale
    foot alternate . . . "
                      That driving

to Chicago we stumbled through poems, shamefaced—nothing
of Crane between us and not much of Pound ("And . . . /
    And . . . " and "Choros nympharum . . . ") and
    fragments of Eliot,

words.
      'The real', o my host—

that you also did laundry, you ended up driving, we sat on the
    bank of the river
at ease and 'in company'.

That since I came home I've been *vomiting memories. Clumsy.
'Stony'.

'Agony'.

*It fell apart there . .

                      (L., on the couch, had read
" 'Stony'. // 'Agony'."
as irony, doggerel; I retreated
to the kitchen "to wash the dishes":
                              the world suddenly
flattened [around me, belongings detached and withdrawn,
    no—estranged, *no*—*disanimate* which had importuned me
for recognition; as from steps, rows of empty benches 'waiting,
    disconsolate'—*no*—on a concourse by a grove of trees at the
    park: I had seen they were flat
as ground, pebbles, etc.] so that I [—all the waiting
was mine] loomed up, with only the usual movements of my hands
    and the play

of water on the shine of the surfaces
buttressing me.
                Lines I had heard as " 'Stony'. // 'Agony'."
  extended, obliquely,
toward—foolhardy
as prayer.

    "If saying *is*
    prayer?
    Then *pray.*"
                —I'd thought something like that twice that day,
both times already safe, standing at the sink rinsing a washed
    plate

as I do [hands closed on opposite edges, rocking and rocking
the surface under warm tapwater])

. . where I couldn't say "lonely."

3)

These things, flat: habit. Shadows.
Chance. The spare

face of the garden the garden
casts of itself across water; an uppermost layer

of pond water glazed with an outermost layer of foliage, bridge,
trees, sky

(but art—the created thing:—rounded? slanted?
leaning?);
       a silence . . .

—The three had been talking, were leaning on the railing

of the Japanese bridge, the arc of the bridge
a darkness below them in the water.
                    Below them

*leaves of nymphéas annexed the surface of the water, mimicked
the plane of the surface of the water, "supine
and contingent"; spread, flat in the second*

*world—the world
ceded, which shudders, is one layer*
                                              —but the leaves
interrupting! overlapping!

                    These things,
upright: prospect; the greening of grass, of leaves,
in the primary. "Lonely" . . .

                              And the figures on the bridge
in the air, audacious

    lilies—

Note on "Mourner's *Kasen* (Mourner's Series)"

A *kasen* is a thirty-six-verse *renga* or "linked poem." In this Japanese poetic form, each verse responds only to the verse prior, creating a series of interlinked or overlapping two-verse poems.

Traditionally composed by a gathering of poets each writing a verse in turn, classical renga alternated three-line and two-line verses (or stanzas) of seventeen and fourteen syllables, respectively—so a "poem set" always comprised two stanzas, five lines, thirty-one syllables. Kasen followed additional rules regarding subject matter, tone, and linking technique that are disregarded here.

Though "Mourner's *Kasen* (Mourner's Series)" follows the kasen's general structure, some three-stanza sets occur, and motifs sometimes extend or recur in ways renga would not allow.

Biographical Note

Carol Snow lives with her husband, David Matchett, in San Francisco, where she was born in 1949. She serves as Administrative Director of Blue Bear School of Music, a nonprofit school teaching rock, pop, jazz, and blues. Ms. Snow first studied poetry with Maurice F. Englander. Her first publication was the long poem "Positions of the Body" in *Antaeus* in 1984.